T0194134

Why Do I Believe?

**"The Heavens Declare the Glory
of God; the Skies Proclaim the
Work of His Hands"**
—*Psalm 19:1*

**Poems
with Comments on My Personal Journey**

Lissette Trahan

WESTBOW
P R E S S®
A DIVISION OF THOMAS NELSON
& ZONDERVAN

WestBow Press books may be ordered through booksellers or by contacting:

WestBow Press
A Division of Thomas Nelson & Zondervan
1663 Liberty Drive
Bloomington, IN 47403
www.westbowpress.com
1 (866) 928-1240

ISBN: 978-1-9736-2768-5 (sc)
ISBN: 978-1-9736-2770-8 (hc)
ISBN: 978-1-9736-2769-2 (e)

Library of Congress Control Number: 2018905499

Print information available on the last page.

WestBow Press rev. date: 05/08/2018

Dedicated to my daughter,

Jennifer Lowery:

Thank you for your support and encouragement.

Your editing is priceless!

And to

Lawrence and Roylynn Trahan:

A family dedicated to
God,
family, and
helping others.

With all my love, praying that all your prayers
be answered.

Fear not for I am with you; be not dismayed, for
I am your God; I will strengthen you, I will
help you, I will uphold you with my righteous right hand.

— Isaiah 41:10 (ESV)

Contents

Poems By Marcie Wert With Comments By Lissette Trahan

Acknowledgments

First and foremost, thanks to God, who inspired me and guided me. My hope is that it will glorify his name.

A thank-you to my daughter, Jennifer Lowery, who has been with me through the whole process, editing and supporting. She was precise in correcting my work lovingly and patiently. I appreciate the hours she spent giving me her invaluable and expert advice.

A very special thank-you to Dixie, Lady Bowen. She wrote a foreword that captured everything my poems were about. I am beyond grateful.

I belong to a blog called atozmomm.com. Atoz has been publishing my poems on her blog for months. Her review and ability with words expressed my heart's desire—that these poems and comments bring everyone closer to God.

Also a thank-you to Marcie Wert and Carolyn Bartlett, who were the first to mention that my poems should be published. Without their encouragement, I would have never tried.

I ended the book with poems that Marcie Wert generously contributed. I hope they inspire you as much as they did me.

The service that I received from James Daniel was priceless. He was the first to contact me from West-Bow-Press. He spent hours patiently teaching me and helping me through the process. His personality is energizing, and what could have been a very difficult part of being published became a pleasure. Thank you, James.

And a thank-you to my wonderful husband of nearly fifty years, Carl Trahan. He provides support and love in anything I do. I cannot imagine life without him.

Lissette Trahan

Foreword

Why Do I Believe? is a tribute to Lissette Trahan's journey in finding Jesus Christ in her world. Her life took her to the jungles of both Venezuela and Belize, where someone left a Bible on the doorstep of her very remote rainforest home. Once Lissette finally opened that book, it changed her life. Within her, she found the words to share through her poetry. And additionally, her comments on and connection to verses put a very special spin on her work. It brings deeper understanding and clarity to all that God has shared with her.

These memorable words give us all insight into ourselves and our paths in life. Lissette's walk in life and with God was not always an easy one. As you will read in her expressive writings, she has weathered many a storm, and in the midst of turmoil, she lost a son when he was at a very young and tender age. Her belief in our Lord and her courage to put her adventures and experiences into the simplest of words in an extraordinary way brings emotion to anyone and everyone.

Read this, and you will get a glimpse of eternity. Lissette's stunning work will give you the power and positivity for your soul to fly and your heart to sing.

Lady Bowen
Belize

Comments on "The Truth"

This poem recounts the beginning of my journey with God. After my eight years of schooling that focused on God morning, noon, and night, I had no idea what God was all about. Throughout those eight years, not once did I see a Bible.

Many years later, while I was living in the jungles of Belize, a lady left me a box full of tapes in front of my door, along with a Bible. I was not interested. It sat unopened for at least three months.

Finally, one day, I did open the box and look in the Bible. It didn't matter that the Bible was given out by a cult. The truth of what I read in the Bible penetrated my soul. And so, as I was seeking the truth, God revealed himself to me. I will never forget that day.

He is the way, the truth, and the life.

He is real.

> Jesus answered, "I am the way, the truth and the life.
> No one comes to the Father except through me."
> —John 14:6 (NIV)

The Truth

I will never forget that day.
So unexpectedly,
You introduced yourself to me
And said, "I am the Way."

I never saw or felt you,
But I knew that you were there.
What joy, what love enveloped me!
I knew then that you cared.

I had been blind; you gave me sight.
I wish I could explain.
The only thing I know for sure
Is that I'm not the same.

So great a love, how can it be?
I asked the question, "Lord, why me?"
My spirit pierced through like a knife;
He died so he could give me life.

O God, my Lord, I worship you.
Is there now something I can do?
I'll tell the world all about you.
You are the way, the life, the truth.

Comment on "What Is with Thee?"

I found out after months of striving and trying to accomplish it all by myself that no matter how right or great the cause, I could not achieve anything unless I depended on Christ. After months of struggling, I surrendered it all to him.

Doors started opening; I would take one step, and another door would open. I started Feed My Sheep, where people were able to help others in need.
(Explanation about Feed My Sheep follows.)

I now have implanted in my heart that things that are impossible in the flesh are more than possible through Christ, who is our strength. The secret is realizing that it is not my strength, but his. Instead of being weary, I was energized. I learned my lesson.

I can do all things through Christ
who strengthens me.
—Philippians 4:13 (NKJV)

What Is with Thee?

As I awake each morning,
My thoughts reach out to you,
A joy within me singing,
"Jesus, I love you too."

With anxious heart I hurry.
There is so much to do!
A dying world you've shown me—
I'll save it, Lord, for you.

I charge with holy fury.
Heathens scatter—it is she
With shield and armor ready.
Lord, aren't you proud of me?

A more true and faithful worker
You'll never find than me,
But I haven't felt your presence.
Lord, I'm feeling so weary.

I feel it in my spirit.
It asks, "What is with thee?"
My God is always waiting;
I rush past indifferently.

Today I'm not so weary,
And some will even say,
"She's never in a hurry."
You see, I've learned to pray.

Comments on "A Part of Me"

My twenty-seven-year-old son died of AIDS. There is no greater loss than the loss of a child, no matter what age. What I can honestly say is that God was closer to me then, like never before or after.

When I was going through the worst of it, I grieved and had my doubts that everything was for my good. Then I turned and praised him and asked forgiveness for ever doubting. That is when he showed me that my son was with him.

My faith grew more powerful than it could ever have become if I had not gone through the tragedy.

He turned my sorrow into joy.

> You will be sorrowful,
> but your sorrow will turn into joy.
> —John 16:20 (ESV)

A Part of Me

"What is this thing called faith?" I ask.
Today so clear and plain to see,
So real, a rock that I can grasp,
Faith has become a part of me.

Then words that paralyze with dread
A mother's heart: "Your son is dead."
O faith that I thought was so strong,
Now that I need you, you are gone.

The morning dawns. What do I feel?
Nothing, yet habit makes me kneel.
I praise you, Lord, and ask you please,
Could you now help my unbelief?

I need a sign that will tell me,
Is he with you eternally?
And then he showed a sign so clear
My sorrow turned to joy with tears.

"What is this thing called faith?" I ask.
I know less now after what's passed,
But this I can say faithfully:
Faith has become a part of me.

Comments on "What Really Matters"

I had come back to the United States. After doing one tour in Belize, I was back living the American dream. I had a beautiful home, and I owned a ladies' accessory shop. I was happy and settled. Then came the shocker: my husband was asked to go back to Belize. I said no way.

A preacher that I had never met came to our town. His name was Jesse Duplantis. I went to a church I had never been in before because I wanted to hear him. He asked the congregation to come forward, which I did. When he came to me, he passed by and then came back to me. I felt like his words came directly from God.

He said, "You will be going to new places. I still have work for you to do. I will be with you."

I obeyed and was so blessed. When you are in God's will, you are never alone.

> Show me your ways, Lord,
> teach me your paths.
> —Psalm 25:4 (NIV)

6

What Really Matters

I've reached another crossroad
In my life today.
Two paths I have before me,
Confusion either way.

Changes that make me tremble,
Choices so hard to make.
My circumstances tell me
My whole life is at stake.

Just when I started feeling
That my life was orderly,
You turned it upside down again.
O Lord, why should it be?

All that I see before me
Is a life so far away
From everything that matters.
O Lord, I want to stay!

And as I turn to go my way,
I glance so fearfully
At that rough and jagged path
That was not meant for me.

Among the thorns and briars
And many deep valleys,
I see someone so very dear
That says "Come, follow me."

Now all I see before me
Is a life so far away
With everything that matters.
Yes, Lord, I'll go your way.

Comment on "It's No Coincidence"

I have lived in third-world countries for at least three decades. My dream was to someday come back to the United States. I now live in the United States, and when I look back at my life, I see that every moment was planned and guided by God.

Living in the jungles of Venezuela and Belize, I know that it was exactly where I was supposed to be. God knew while I was being formed in my mother's womb that I was his and what I would do with my life.

I wasn't always obedient, but when I look back now, I see so clearly that when I was, I felt the peace, joy, and love that he promises in the Bible.

I rejoice knowing I belong to him.

> I knew you before I formed you in your mother's
> womb. Before you were born I set you apart.
> —Jeremiah 1:5 (NLT)

It's No Coincidence

I know it's no coincidence
I live just where I do.
You've planned my life and know my ways.
You know me through and through.

When trials come along the way,
As they so often do,
I know it's no coincidence
I feel so close to you.

The joy that soars within me
At the mention of your name—
I know it's no coincidence
Through death my life you claimed.

When nothing is the matter
But I still feel so cast down,
I know it's no coincidence
Scriptures with love abound.

A peace that I don't understand
Yet flows through all of me—
I know it's no coincidence
You promised it would be.

And then sometimes I wonder
Lord, why do you love me?
I know it's no coincidence
That I happen to be.

With love and joy you formed me
And knew all I would be.
You see, it's no coincidence
That you created me.

Comments on "Where Have You Been?"

There have been days that I pray, that I search, that I thirst for more. It all seems void and empty. Each time I have realized that God has always been there.

I spend time with him because I love him, praising him, worshiping him. Not because I want something, but because he wants to have a relationship with me.

I have learned to talk to him. He, the God of the universe, desires for me to have a relationship with him.

It overwhelms me!

Behold, I stand at the door and knock.
If anyone hears my voice and opens the door,
I will come in to him and eat with him, and he with me.
—Revelation 3:20 (ESV)

Where Have You Been?

Early do I seek him
With a cry deep from within.
My prayer was just to know him;
Why do I search again?

My Bibles, books, and tapes
I frantically search through.
One glimpse, one sign this day, O Lord,
That's all I ask of you

You said I'd never thirst again;
Why, then, my panting heart?
One look was all you gave me then;
Now how to live apart?

With tears of desperation,
I get down on my knees.
"My God, have you forgotten
Your promises to me?"

And then, ever so gently,
I hear deep from within,
"Your prayer was just to know me.
Why do you search again?"

The day I opened up the door
And asked him to come in,
He had been waiting there for me.
My God, where have I been?

Comment on "Promises"

God's promises are forever. He can be trusted to keep his promises. Many times he has kept me from failing. Many times I have said thank you, knowing that it came from him. He has comforted me when I was desperate.

He never said there would be no pain or sorrow, but he has been right by my side when I needed him. He gave me strength when I was weak. He was faithful when I wasn't. I have never felt judged. I have felt loved. I have felt forgiven. He will never leave me or forsake me.

I thank you, Jesus, for the gift and promise of the Comforter, the Holy Spirit. Because you provided that promise, I will live with you eternally.

I still have the sin nature, but I am not defeated. That is the victory of the cross.

> For all have sinned, and come short of the glory of God.
> —Romans 3:23 (KJV)

> For I am convinced that neither death nor life, neither angels nor demons, neither the present nor the future, nor any powers, neither height nor depth, nor anything else in all creation, will be able to separate us from the love of God that is in Christ Jesus our Lord.
> —Romans 8:38 (NIV)

Promises

God, I am so sorry
I have offended thee.
It's always the same story,
These sins that beset me.

I cry out so sincerely,
Confess, and promise you
These sins I lay before thee
Again I'll never do.

Then comes a bright new morning.
I praise and worship you.
My sins have been forgiven;
I'll start my life anew.

So here I am this evening.
What did I do today?
I thoroughly examine.
What did I have to say?

Alas, the same old story!
I have offended thee.
I come again so humbly,
Knowing you will hear me.

As I kneel down before you,
I realize gratefully
Your promises to me
Are not like mine to thee.

Comment on "We Perish, Lord"

I am eighty-two years old, and in all my lifetime, I have never seen such immorality, violence, and lack of compassion as I see today. When I listen to the news, it is depressing. When I try to see a movie, it usually starts out with violence or sex.

I ask myself why? What is the real cause? Some people blame the TV, the media, but it only follows the demand.

I think back to when I was growing up. A lot has changed. Having sex before marriage is common. A family sitting together to pray—does that ever happen anymore?

God is missing; family is missing. Will it ever change?

> For the time will come when people will
> not put up with sound doctrine. Instead, to suit their own
> desires, they will gather around them a great number of
> teachers to say what their itching ears want to hear.
> —2 Timothy 4:3 (NIV)

We Perish, Lord

I looked around the world today:
Chaos, confusion, disarray,
The pain and sorrow, hurt and care.
"Lord, what is happening out there?"

What's happened to the unity
That stood for home and family?
Where did the love and honor go,
A child to parents used to show?

Abortion, drugs, adultery
Are words this generation knows.
Corruption's all that I can see.
"Lord, are you really in control?"

The faith and hope and charity
This nation had and used to share,
Where has it gone? It used to be!
We perish, Lord. Why don't you care?

This world you died and suffered for,
Does it not need you anymore?
I fear that it's too blind to see.
Are we repeating history?

Son of David, have mercy on me.
Incline your ear; please hear my plea.
I know nothing is too hard for you,
For they don't know, Lord, what they do.

Pour forth your spirit. Awake the dead.
Those stony hearts will turn instead.
Your grace and love will mightily
Do miracles, Lord, as you did for me.

Comment on "This Friend You've Given Me"

The most essential part of a friendship is trust. To be able to share your feelings, your thoughts, without fear of judgment or criticism. To love no matter what happens in your life. To be encouraging, forgiving, dependable.

But most importantly, a friend accepts you as you are. And remember to have a friend, you have to be a friend.

If you are lucky enough to find one that you can pray with, you are fortunate indeed.

A friend loves at all times,
and a brother is born for a time of adversity.
—Proverbs 17:17 (NIV)

This Friend You've Given Me

The many gifts and blessings, Lord,
That you have given me
Fill me with thanks and gratitude
And love that praises thee,

But there's one thing above the rest
I treasure specially.
I hardly know how to express;
It means so much to me.

When sorrow strikes, I call her.
She hears my "Woe is me"
And lets me talk forever,
And then says, "Let's pray, shall we?"

You knew all she would have to be
To get along with me,
So then you gave her patience,
love, and humility.

But what I cherish most of all
Is the ability
To share the love we have for you
With this friend
You've given me.

Comment on "A Sinner"

One of my favorite stories in the Bible is the story of David. David had many qualities described in his own writings.

He was trusting:

> The Lord is my light and my salvation—whom shall I fear? (Psalm 27:1 NIV)

He was loving:

> I love you, O Lord, my strength. (Psalm 18:1 NIV)

He was repentant:

> For the sake of your name, Lord, forgive my iniquity, though it is great. (Psalm 25:11 NIV)

It shows the grace and love of God. Anything is forgiven if I repent. I am a sinner, and there is great comfort in knowing that I have a God who is greater than any sin. What I learned is that no matter what problems I have or how hard life becomes, I accept it, never doubting that it will be for my good.

Like David, I want to become a woman after God's own heart.

> I have found David the son of Jesse,
> a man after mine own heart, which shall fulfill
> all my will.
> —Acts 13:22 (KJV)

A Sinner

There is a Bible story about David, the king.
Mostly when talked about, it is about his sin.
What I see is a story of grace and restoration.
Rejoicing, I thank God there is no separation.

David

A man after God's own heart:
He was the greatest sinner,
And yet you called him that.
What did he do? He loved you,
Repenting, for a start,
Accepting what sin did to him.
He never turned his back.

Lord, let me learn a lesson
From this man who stole your heart.

Comment on "Why Do I Believe?"

I look at our small planet. It is the size of a grain of sand compared to the universe. How can I not believe that there is a designer, a God holding it all together? Maybe the big bang is true, but even then, where did the materials for the big bang come from? It is easier to believe that there is a loving God that planned us, that planned this beautiful earth.

This is the title of this book. One night I looked up. I really saw the stars, the galaxies, and the universe. How could I not be convinced?

I can only offer my wonder and awe. When I consider the vastness of the universe in which our tiny planet spins in existence, I am humbled.

I was a skeptic for so long, until I opened the Bible. There I found Jesus—then it all made sense.

> The heavens declare the glory of God;
> The skies proclaim the work of His hands.
> —Psalm 19:1 (NIV)

Why Do I Believe?

One verse for me was all it took.
Why did I wait so long to look?

The answer is not hard to find;
My problem was I did not seek.
Without him, I had made it fine,
But one day, I did take a peek.

And there it was in Psalm 19:
"The heavens declare the glory of God;
The skies proclaim the work of his hands."

Was that verse always there for me?
Today, I feel God made it mine.

In this world, what do we mostly see?
The universe, stars, galaxies,
An order that could never be—
It was right there, but I didn't see.

Reading more deeply in God's Word,
I found the truth I had not heard:
A love so great, he gave his life.
He thought that I was worth the price.

His resurrection was proof for me.

Comment on "Joy"

The joy of belonging to Christ—there are no words that can express the feeling. The whole purpose of his coming to take away my sins in order to bring me joy—the joy of salvation.

When I am filled with his love and let him direct my life, everything seems to fall into place. Besides joy are peace, love, and the knowledge that there is nothing in this world too hard to overcome.

Jesus is a friend, always there, ready to listen, ready to help, wanting what is best for me. He is the Holy Spirit dwelling in me, always with me.

On him I can always depend.

> May the God of hope fill you with all joy and
> peace as you trust in him, so that you may overflow
> with hope by the power of the Holy Spirit.
> —Romans 15:13 (NIV)

Joy

When I surrendered my life to you,
Little did I know what it would do,
How much joy that it would bring
When you erased all of my sin.

A joy that nothing can take away,
Powerless to touch, it's there to stay.
No grief, no pain, no sorrow, no loss—
That is the victory of the cross.

I still have days where things are shattered,
Days I have tears and nothing matters,
But even then, I know he is there,
Loving and caring; I don't despair.

Human relationships come to an end,
Even the ones we call "best friend."

There is one friend nothing destroys.
He is the reason for my joy.
I can't imagine life without him.
He is with me through lose or win

On Jesus, my Savior, I can depend,
My friend until the end.

Comment on "Prayer"

For me prayer is talking to God and listening to God. It is a response to God inviting me to spend time with him. He wants to have a relationship, and prayer helps develop my relationship with him. What I yearn and long for in this life is having that relationship with him. Prayer is intimacy with God.

I can go to him with problems, with confessions, and with my gratitude. He will never tire of hearing from me. He loves me and knows my name.

Praying isn't always easy. When I have sinned and not confessed it seems like my prayers are futile. But it isn't that God is not listening.

In the Bible, it says, *"You will seek me and find me when you seek me with all your heart" (Jeremiah 29:13 NIV).*

I was seeking when I felt his presence. Seeking is a way of praying. God knows what I need or what I am going to say. I wasn't eloquent; I just cried out, wanting to know him.

> In my distress I called to the Lord;
> I cried to my God for help.
> From his temple he heard my voice;
> my cry came before him, into his ears.
> —Psalm 18:6 (NIV)

Prayer

Knock and I will answer;
Seek and you will find.
Why does it seem harder
To talk to you sometimes?

Then I stop to examine
What have I done today:
Have I committed any sin
Getting in the way?

The only time I find it hard
Is when I move away.
Make sure I stay on guard.
Please help me, Lord, to stay.

I know words do not matter.
You see right through my heart.
You know what I am about to say
Even before I start.

I thank you, God, for listening—
Praying day or night.

Comment on "Sin"

The sins that I regret the most are the ones I committed after knowing Jesus, after feeling his love. I know that I am forgiven, but I remember being shocked and heartbroken. I hated my sin and my weakness.

I was born again, but it didn't eliminate that sin nature that I was born with. That sin nature will be a part of me while I am in this body. Through Adam, I inherited it. I was born guilty with no hope.

> But God loved me so much that he did something incredible. He sent his Son, Jesus, who led a sinless life. It was his innocent blood that saved me. His sacrifice gave me the greatest gift of all, the Holy Spirit, the Comforter. It guides me, it convicts me, and it teaches me the way.

Before I knew God, I sinned; after I knew God, I sinned. The difference is that I hate to sin. I ask forgiveness. Sin has no hold on me.

No more a slave to sin, I am free.

> For God so loved the world that he gave His
> one and only son, that whoever believes in Him
> should not perish but have eternal life.
> —John 3:16 (NIV)

Sin

What is this thing that we call sin?
The word alone, it makes me cringe.
To hurt the one that died for me,
It was my sin there on that tree.

Your Word says we all have sinned.
Without the cross, I'd be condemned.
It was the cross that set me free,
The blood that you shed on that tree.

It was the love you had for me,
A love that I can feel today.
A comforter always with me,
It guides and teaches me the way.

Sin, now where is your victory?
Sin, now where is your sting?
Your death turned into liberty.
Rejoicing, I will sing.

Jesus, my Lord and Savior,
How can I show my gratitude?

Comment on "How Can That Be?"

How have I gone astray? My biggest sin has been to ignore him. I get busy, I get distracted, and I become too involved with the things of this world. However, when I turn back to him, He is there with his arms open to receive me. God is so full of mercy and grace. Even when I am unfaithful, his love never fails.

All of us in this human journey are seeking something—seeking God, seeking purpose in life. Temptations, sin, and problems will always be there. When I turn to Jesus is when I realize *he is the only thing that matters.*

> For now we see only a reflection as in a mirror; then
> we shall see face to face. Now I know in part; then
> I shall know fully, even as I am fully known.
> —1 Corinthians 13:12 (NIV)

How Can That Be?

O God, so many years have slipped away,
Years where I know I've gone astray.
You then revealed yourself to me.
Sin, it is gone—how can that be?

Whatever path that I went down,
You pursued me all along.
Your love disarmed me so completely.
Now my desire is just to please thee.

Whenever I remember how faithful you have been,
It brings tears to my eyes; I know that I have sinned.
Confess my sins—where do I start?
How could I've kept you far apart?

If I could start again, would I live differently?
But I know sin would be there.
O Lord, how can that be?

Then I remember Jesus, who gave his life for me.
He came down here to save me so that I could be free.
Those sins I was enslaved to are not a part of me.
I am a new creation, a proof that all can see.

Jesus is the answer. "That is how it can be."

Comment on "Mary"

Of all the poems that I have composed, "Mary" is one of my favorites. There is so much to admire. She was a teenager, espoused to a man she loved, and about to embark on her life.

Because of the courage and faith of a teenage girl, we have Jesus. She knew the risks involved in what she was asked to do. Her belief, trust, and love for God gave her the strength. She never doubted.

I try to picture myself living in that generation. What would I have done?

I don't know.

> And Mary said, "Behold the handmaid of
> the Lord; be it unto me according to thy word."
> And the angel departed from her.
> —Luke 1:38 (KJV)

Mary

Have you ever thought of Mary,
What she was told that day?
It must have been so scary
To have been told that way.

"You are to be a mother," Gabriel announced to her.
"How? I am still a virgin" was how Mary replied.
"The Holy Ghost shall come on thee" is what it says she heard.
She must have been in wonder, completely mystified.

Then came more bewilderment; Gabriel was not yet through:
"You will bring forth a son; he'll be the Son of God."
What trust God had in Mary! He knew what she would do.
"Behold the maiden of the Lord," she said without a doubt.

Mary already had a spouse. What was to be her fate?
In those days, it was a crime; she could be stoned to death.
When God plans your life, you know he'll keep you safe.
Mary could have said no but willingly said yes.

Mary said yes to a future, not knowing what it would be.
I want to follow that example and let God work through me.

Comment on "The Way"

I was a skeptic for such a long time. I was in my thirties when I first opened a Bible. I have told you how it happened to come to my doorstep. That by itself was a miracle.

God's plans stand firm forever. His eyes were fixed on me. Nothing could prevent his purposes from being fulfilled.

God went to many lengths to show me that he loved me, to show me that he wanted me. I have no doubt that if I had not decided to read his Word, he would have found another way to introduce himself.

God never gives up on us. He will knock until the very end. He is so ready to forgive, to make you his child.

> Behold, I stand at the door and knock.
> If anyone hears my voice and opens the door,
> I will come into him and eat with him, and
> he with me.
> —Revelation 3:20 (ESV)

The Way

Somebody said, "Just seek and find."
It seemed like such a waste of time.
I just really didn't care
If there was anything out there.

What I found and didn't know:
God wouldn't easily let me go.
He pursued me with his love.
How to resist? Where else to go?

Only he knew what it would take.
How could I know what was at stake?
The love he showed me was the key.
I opened the door so cautiously.

Why would he want to talk to me?
I'd treated him so horribly.
I humbly asked him to come in.
Would he forgive me all my sins?

He'd knocked and waited patiently,
This God who had created me;
Then so amazingly,
I felt his love envelop me.

My love just grew by leaps and bounds.

I felt him rejoicing with me.

I had been found!

Comment on "Prophecy"

Prophecy was what proved to me that the Bible was the Word of God.

Prophecy is a message inspired by God. These messages were foretold hundreds of years before they happened.

When I first began to read the Bible, I was in a place where there were no Bible studies or churches. There was so much I did not understand. When I think back, I can see that the Holy Spirit led me and taught me. I came back with the knowledge of Jesus and the Holy Spirit.

I am so grateful for the Bible studies and churches that I was finally able to go to. Learning that the Old Testament and the New Testament are all connected opened my eyes even more.

I wonder if there are others who had that problem when they first started? I can sympathize with anyone who first opens the Bible and has no one to instruct him or her, or to talk to about it.

The following is one of my favorite prophecies.

> Therefore the Lord himself will give you a sign:
> The virgin will conceive and give birth to a son,
> and will call him Immanuel.
> —(Isaiah 7:14 NIV)

Prophecy

The more I read the Bible,
More clearly I can see
The miracle of prophecy
That leads me straight to thee.

So many years neglected,
At first I could not see
How it was all connected:
The old, the new,
And what's to be.

In searching the Old Testament,
I see the New fulfilled.
His Word is all one statement.
How great is prophecy!

It shows me that his Word
From Genesis to end
All points to my Redeemer.
How can I make amends?

How did I miss the miracle
Your Word was there to see—
A beautiful love letter
Made especially for me?

Comment on "How Did It Happen?"

There is this beautiful earth with all its wonders. The miracle of the Holy Spirit. The Bible. Then there is life. The human body, a treasure of mysteries that still confounds doctors and scientists.

I don't believe in coincidences. I believe God plans every second of our lives. I stay focused; I stay alert, watching to see what he will do next in my life. What I am sure of is that whatever he does will be for my good.

We have an awesome God!

> For since the creation of the world God's invisible qualities—his eternal power and divine nature—have been clearly seen, being understood from what has been made, so that people are without excuse.
> Romans 1:20 (NIV)

How Did It Happen?

Blessings so many and so great—
Where do I start? How to relate?

When I awake, the sun is there.
How did it happen? Do I care?
Do I ever stop to think
If one day it was out of sync?

Seasons follow each other in order.
Tides ebb and flow. The sun rises and sets.
I look at the world, and I have to say,
"How did it happen, this great display?"

Then there is life; how did it happen?
Humans have never a life created.
I know that there had to be a beginning.
Without a God? I would debate it.

The fact of the world drives me to God—
The order, the detail.
I stay in awe.

Thank you, Lord. I am so humbled.
You've shown me so much, and I still stumble,
But the victory I have no one can take.

I have faith.

Comment on "One Question"

While living in Belize, I was listening to a preacher from Puerto Rico. I always felt light-hearted after his sermons. He had a way of taking some of the parables and seeing the irony and humor in them. This poem was inspired by one of his sermons.

I am so grateful for the Bible and the answers that it has given me. I thank God for it every day.

> May these words of my mouth and this
> meditation of my heart
> be pleasing in your sight,
> Lord, my Rock and my Redeemer.
> —Psalm 19:14 (NIV)

One Question

As I was watching worship,
I heard the preacher say,
"And now, how can I help you?
What's on your heart today?

"If you had just one question
That you could ask the Lord...?"
I came right to attention.
That really struck a chord.

What is it like in heaven?
Why did you make Adam?
Why did you make me?
Why did you let Satan
Overcome so easily?

What about the angels?
Surely they get lonely!
They're not made in your image,
As you made me to be.

What about eternity?
It's really hard to see
How it had no beginning,
And the end will never be.

So many hours I studied
And realized finally,
Your Word has all the answers
I need in this journey.

Comment on "Christmas"

Christmas! How to explain the greatest event in the history of humankind? God came to earth as Jesus—a small baby, poor and vulnerable.

> Almighty, powerful God, who created the universe, who created you and me, became one of us. He gave us his Son, Jesus, knowing that he would be sacrificed so that we could have the Holy Spirit and salvation.

I will never understand that great a love. What I do understand is that God has not forgotten us. That is why Christmas is also a time of joy, a time to celebrate, and a time to give glory to God.

> Praise be to the Lord, the God of Israel, because He
> has come to His people and redeemed them.
> —Luke 1:68 (NIV)

Christmas

When Jesus was born in Bethlehem,
Very few knew what it meant.
Today, I know more than they did then—
History's greatest event.

It is still hard for me to grasp
How deep a love he had to have
To leave the life he had with God,
Knowing the plan—what it would cost.

He knew we would not survive
Unless he came and paid the price.
It had to be a sinless life,
The Lamb of God, the sacrifice.

At Christmastime, as we reflect
What God did when he sent his Son,
How could I possibly neglect
To love,
To praise,
That Christmas, Christ agreed to come?

He left us the great gift of love.

Comment on "Hope"

Without hope, life loses its meaning. In this life, you need something to hope for. My hope is believing in Jesus Christ, my Lord and Savior. Hope is belief in God who can be trusted to keep his promises.

It was hope that kept me seeking.

It was hope and his grace that made me open that Bible and start reading it with an open heart.

It was hope that gave me the faith I have today.

The Bible is the biggest gift that God left us. It is a miracle; it is a love letter to us. It proves itself.

Wherever there is assurance of hope, there is faith. I am saved by grace through hope. Hope gives me the power to live courageously, to be all that Christ has called me to be. Hope gives me that certainty that what is promised in his Word is true—hope, then faith, which in turn produces peace. When I have peace, I have joy.

The greatest joy is that I will live with him eternally. On that, I have faith.

> May the God of hope fill you with all
> joy and peace as you trust in him,
> so that you may overflow with hope
> by the power of the Holy Spirit.
> —Romans 15:13 (NIV)

Hope

The greatest hope that Christ gives me:
To live with him eternally.
Because he died, I will arise.
Jesus fulfilled that sacrifice.

Hope is having faith to believe.
The Bible proved it all to me.
It is all guaranteed and sealed.
Someday it will be revealed.

Without hope, what would life be?
Days when hope feels far away—
That is where faith is what I see.
It is hope that helps me pray.

For who hopes for what he sees?
Instead, I wait patiently.
I know the plans God has for me:
A future of welfare, hope, and peace.

Today, I have the Holy Spirit,
A gift and taste of what's to be,
A hope of what I will inherit.
Adopted, I've become family.

Comment on "God Is Good"

Life can be hard, but God is good. I have experienced God's goodness in my life when I was going through the worst kind of grief. I doubted his goodness. Then came his compassion, so great a love that my tears turned to joy.

Whatever he does has a purpose. No matter what I am going through, I trust him. His mercy will follow. He is my creator, he loves me, and every breath I take is given to me by him.

Living in a world that is constantly changing, it is comforting to know God will always be the same. He does not change. God is good.

> Jesus Christ is the same yesterday and today and forever.
> —Hebrews 13:8 (NIV)

> And we know that in all things God
> works for the good of those who love
> him, who have been called according
> to his purpose.
> —Romans 8:28 (NIV)

God Is Good

God is good.
Miracles are everywhere,
Cannot be misunderstood;
I just have to be aware.

There is the miracle of birth.
Every time a child is born,
I am amazed as I observe
How perfectly he or she is formed.

What is this feeling called love?
That is something I didn't learn.
A bit of God placed in me,
Another miracle confirmed.

Each morning, as I awake,
I see the sun; what did it take?
Another miracle I see,
Once more aware that it is he.

When I look up at the stars,
I see the master of the universe.
I feel a burst right in my heart.
Another miracle occurs.

Hundreds of books that it would take
To explain how that "God is good";
You never cease to amaze.
I worship and I praise.

Comment on "Repentance"

Repentance is a change of heart. It is an inward response. It is also a change of actions. Repentance is a gift of God. He draws me to him; he chose me. I did not earn it. I didn't change because it was a duty; I changed because of his love for me.

Receiving the gift of the Holy Spirit opened my eyes and changed my heart. Do I still sin? Yes, but I lose my peace and run back to him, knowing he will accept me.

> You know I am mortal but you love me. You know I am flawed, but you redeemed me. You know I am not perfect but you sent Jesus as the perfect sacrifice to save me.

Knowing God began with a sense of sin, What it did by putting Jesus on a cross, it opened my eyes to the horror of what it could do.

> No one can come to me unless the
> Father who sent me draws them, and
> I will raise them up at the last day.
> —John 6:44 (NIV)

Repentance

The beginning of understanding God
Began when I was convicted of sin.
I confessed so many thoughts,
Repenting for all that I had been.

The seed of love entered my heart,
That spirit of love, never to part.
I was forgiven by God's grace.
With gratitude and joy, I praised.

My way into the kingdom of God
Was with sorrow and repentance.
God was there with all his love.
I felt comfort and acceptance.

I have come to understand
Repentance is a gift of God.
It is not something that I planned;
God chose me from the start.

In spite of all, I still offend,
But I know that when I say,
"Forgive me, Lord; I have sinned,"
He forgives me every day.

Comment on "Pride"

Pride can sneak up on you even when you are doing a good deed. I always ask myself, "Am I proud because I am so good at it or because it benefits another?" Pride can keep us from admitting sin. It is like a self-made person in love with him- or herself as creator. Being proud of a job well done is different from the pride that keeps us away from God.

Boasting about myself? Not giving God the glory? How foolish. What do I have that I have not received? My goal in life is to do God's work. Anything else is work in vain.

To be humble brings God's grace.

> In his pride the wicked man does not
> seek him; in his thoughts there is no room
> for God.
> —Psalm 10:4 (NIV)

Pride

Pride—an abomination to the Lord.
I wish I wasn't guilty,
But I've been there before,
Feeling so unworthy,
My peace being destroyed.

I repented and confessed
I have offended you.
Those sins that you detest,
You know they hurt me too.

With pride comes disgrace.
Humility brings God's grace.
I will not my God forsake
For someone's earthly praise.

The Word is full of warnings
Too serious to ignore.
Lord, help me wake each morning.
Today, pride I'll abhor.

I know the days I honor you
I feel that inner peace.
Why would I let pride destroy
What you have given me?

I need to pray that I don't fall—
An easy thing to do.
The devil won't come near me
If I'm glorifying you.

Comment on "Closer Than I Think"

There are mornings when I wake up depressed. My life doesn't seem to have a reason. It is the same old same old. I go through the daily motions: brush my teeth, get dressed, and get my coffee.

Then I take a peek outside. The sun is shining. Birds are singing. I am alive. I turn my thoughts to God, and my mood lightens with gratitude.

He is always there waiting for us to think about him, to talk to him. He never makes me feel guilty; he just waits, knowing that he can meet my every need.

Remember, he is closer than you think.

> Behold, I am with you always,
> even to the end of the age.
> —Matthew 28:20 (WEB)

Closer Than I Think

There are days that can be hard;
Aches and pains don't let me start.
That is when I feel you there.
You are closer than I think.

Such distraction with a prayer!
Lord, your presence is not there.
That is when I am aware
You are closer than I think.

When I'm feeling so cast down,
Lord, I feel I can't go on;
That is when I feel you there.
You are closer than I think.

When my life has gone all wrong,
Lord, I'm feeling all alone;
That is when I feel you there.
You are closer than I think.

I have learned to meditate.
It is all about your grace.
The answer is right there.
That is what it takes.

Comment on "Who Is This Man?"

Who is Jesus Christ? First and foremost, he is God. He is the creator of all, the author of life. He left his heavenly throne to become human. He came with one mission: to lead a sinless life so that he could be the Lamb of God, a sacrifice for my sins.

He was crucified and resurrected. He left me the gift of the Holy Spirit. Because of him, I will live eternally. Above all, he showed me what love is. We must all answer this question sooner or later.

Who is this man?

He is my Savior.

> For God so loved the world that he gave his only Son,
> that whoever believes in him shall not perish
> but have eternal life.
> —John 3:16 (ESV)

Who Is This Man?

Who is this man who changed history?
Even the times are known as BC–AD.
He left his mighty power to become like us.
From being God to human—that is love.

He came with a plan to save humanity.
We had no hope, dominated by sin.
Fire, wailing, and gnashing of teeth:
That is what our future would have been.

Jesus is the man who changed history.

Just as all humankind was a part of Adam's sin,
Jesus's sinless death saved humanity.
His death and resurrection reversed everything.
He became like us so we might become like him.

Now we have to choose between death or life,
The kingdom of darkness or the kingdom of light.

He came to earth as an innocent lamb.
How can I show him how grateful I am?
His love for us I will never understand.
Before he came he had it all planned.

Jesus, the man who changed history:
His one selfless act gave us eternity.

Comment on "By My Side"

I often wonder what I would be like if Jesus were by my side. Would I be ashamed of where I am, of what I am doing, of what I am saying? Would I make the same choices when facing my day-to-day problems? Or would I be a pretender? I want to be all he wants me to be, but so many times I fail.

I know I would ask him to forgive me for the many times I have offended him and thank him for the many blessings. I would tell him all my problems and let him help me with the decisions.

I have the miracle of the Holy Spirit living in me and beside me, teaching me and guiding me. He will never leave me. He is in me and for me. I don't have to wonder. He is by my side.

> For God is working in you, giving you the desire
> and the power to do what pleases him.
> —Philippians 2:13 (NIV)

By My Side

If Jesus was by my side,
How would I act? What would I say?
I know so much I'd try to hide.
I would act a different way.

Thinking back on my life's journey,
Lord, I have many regrets.
Sins that make me feel unworthy
I do humbly confess.

What would he have to say to me?
He came to earth to let me see—
To show me, Lord, what I could be,
Guiding me to glory.

He became like me
So I could become like him.
He showed me love.
Why do I sin?

I'm so grateful for his blood.
Day by day, it cleanses me.
I feel loved and never judged.
By your side, I know I'm free.

Comment on "Hunger"

I have found out, going through life, that if I am not hungry or thirsty for God, there is something wrong with me spiritually. Hungering for God is that desire that we have when we want to get closer to him, know him more, and have a closer relationship with him.

But I find I am never satisfied. The more I long for him, the more I yearn for him, the more I want. It is like an insatiable thirst. When I read the book of Psalms, I see where David had that same yearning and longing, forever crying out to God. God called him a man after his own heart.

Hungering, yearning, longing brings action. God does bring joy and contentment but leaves me wanting more.

> You are my God, earnestly I seek you;
> I thirst for you, my whole being longs for you,
> in a dry and parched land where there is no water.
> I have seen you in the sanctuary and
> beheld your power and your glory.
> Because your love is better than life,
> my lips will glorify you.
> —Psalm 63:1–3 (NIV)

Hunger

I hunger, O Lord, for more of you.
You gave me a taste of what you can do.
Now why does it feel like you withdrew?
Your promises tell me that is not true.

The more you reveal yourself to me,
The more I want, the more I need.
I am never satisfied. I am never appeased.
A life without you—I cannot breathe.

Forgive me, O Lord! I am so blind.
You've shown me your love again and again.
I know you are there; it depends on me.
Your Word clearly says, "I am with you always."

Why would I think that you are gone?
You have been with me all life long.

As I look at the beauty of each day,
I see your presence in display.

Comment on "A Woman after My Heart"

My desire is not for fame, nor wealth, nor love, nor health. My heart's desire is that when I see Jesus face-to-face, he would say "Here is a woman after my own heart." What does it mean to be a person after God's own heart?

I read the story of David, and it gives me hope. David was a sinner, but he was humble—he admitted his sin and asked forgiveness. David loved God and cried out to God, and the consequence of his sin did not turn him from God.

Most importantly, David never ignored God. I know that is the way to God's heart. Love does not ignore.

> I have found David the son of Jesse, a man after
> mine own heart, which shall fulfill all my will.
> —Acts 13:22 (KJV)

A Woman after My Heart

One of the things I don't know for sure:
what is my heart's desire?

Is it wealth? Is it fame? Is it love? Is it health?
What is it I require?

When I get this feeling of emptiness, what is it, Lord, that I want?

I pray and I ask, "God, what is wrong?"
waiting for some response.

I already know what the problem is. That
little voice comes from within,

Asking me where I've been.

It happens again and again. When I
ignore Jesus, my closest friend,

I know that my real desire is to never be apart.

Someday, I want to hear the Lord say,
"You're a woman after my own heart."

Comment on "The Word"

The Bible is God's Word to us. It is like reading a love letter to us from the creator of the universe. I didn't understand this right away, but I kept reading. I kept on seeking to know more. Once the truth penetrates, you can never let it go.

The Bible is the most important book on the earth. The most important book ever written. It has been proven to be accurate. Many have tried to disprove it and failed. Discoveries keep coming up verifying and supporting it.

It changed my life. It introduced me to history's most important figure, Jesus.

Read this book, and your life will change.

So faith comes from hearing,
and hearing through the word of Christ.
—Romans 10:17 (ESV)

The Word

The power of your Word created the world.
I opened the book, the truth finally heard.
A love letter to me—we call it the Bible.
With instructions so clear, it is my survival.

The Bible revealed God, Jesus in action.
I felt his love; I felt his passion.
Reading his Word, I found the truth.
My life has changed; how much more proof?

So many years not knowing the Word,
I am a true witness of what it can do.
I had been told, but I had not heard
His sacrifice, his love. My life was renewed.

The power of your Word keeps the world in order.
God left us that Word. God left us that power.
Your Word says to go and preach in the world.
How I lead my life speaks louder than words.

Your Word became flesh.
You became my Savior.

Comment on "Matthew"

Matthew, an apostle of Jesus, shows a great example of what it is to believe Jesus. When Jesus said, "Follow me," Matthew left his profitable career that provided wealth—for poverty and uncertainty. He knew that he would never be able to go back to that life.

Something about Jesus must have given him the courage and belief that what he was leaving behind was no comparison to what he was gaining. Did he know that he was abandoning the pleasures of this world to gain eternity?

I wonder how many of us today would be willing to do that, to take that risk.

> As Jesus went on from there, he saw a man named
> Matthew sitting at the tax collector's booth. "Follow me,"
> he told him, and Matthew got up and followed him.
> —Matthew 9:9 (NIV)

Matthew

Jesus came by and said, "Come follow me."
Matthew left it all. What did he see?

He left it all, but he took one thing:
His ability and talent he had with a pen.
The impact his words had in the ages to come
There was no way he could have known.

Matthew must have had an ache in his heart.
He was hated by all; his life was void.
Something about Jesus he could not disregard
When Jesus said to him, "Come follow me."

Of all the disciples, Matthew gave up the most.
Peter and Andrew could go back to their boats.
Matthew gave all he had, believing in Christ.
He trusted, surrendered, and gave up his life.

When Jesus said, "Come follow me,"
Without hesitation, Matthew agreed.
With one action, in one moment of time,
He made a decision. It was God's design.

In the Bible, we have the first teachings of Jesus
Written by Matthew.

This story of Matthew is a lesson for me.

Comment on "Why Do I Worry?"

Worry seems to be a part of human nature. I can say, "I will not worry," but when the problems come, I do worry. Worry is such a waste of time. It doesn't fix the problem. When I worry, I am not trusting God.

Even knowing that doesn't keep me from worrying.

God tells us not to worry, to give him all our concerns. I know deep in my heart that there is nothing I am going through that he is not attentive to. When I go to him in prayer, he promises to give me the peace that "passeth understanding" (Philippians 4:6–7).

What a wonderful promise. Peace is what erases worry. Trusting what he promises is the answer.

Casting all your anxiety on him, because he cares for you.
—1 Peter 5:7 (NIV)

Do not be anxious about anything, but in everything
by prayer and supplication with thanksgiving let your
requests be made known to God. And the peace
of God, which passeth understanding, will guard
your hearts and your minds in Christ Jesus.
—Philippians 4:6–7 (ESV)

Why Do I Worry?

To trust you, O Lord, is to say I love you.
I wish I could say that I always do.
To say I don't worry would not be the truth.
The desire of my heart is to always please you.

Trusting is easy when things go my way,
But oh, how I stumble when things go astray!
You prove your faithfulness time after time.
Instead of thanking you, I ask for a sign.

I think back at my life and all I can see.
Why did I worry? You were right there by me.
A life without worry—how great that would be!
A life without worry—then I'd be free!

Your love kept me always from falling apart.
I know I can trust you with all of my heart.

You keep my paths straight.
You guide me through life.
My life I now celebrate,
Worry or not.

Comment on "His Blood"

The Bible is clear. We are separated from God because of our sin. Yet the Bible tells Christians to come boldly into his presence. What made the difference? The Bible says,

> *Now you in Christ Jesus you who were once far off have been made near by the blood of Jesus. (Ephesians 2:13 NIV)*

The blood of Jesus does not just do away with sin, It saved me. It is the blood of Jesus that makes me acceptable to the Father. It was his blood that removed the veil, that removed the penalty of sin.

Because of the blood of Jesus, I can pour out my heart to him. I can cast my cares on him and talk to him day or night.

Because of the blood of Jesus, my sins are forgiven. Just as the blood of the lamb delivered the Hebrews from the angel of death in Egypt, so Christ's blood delivers me from judgment.

Because of the blood of Jesus, I have a new relationship with God.

No guilt, no shame:

> In him we have redemption through his blood,
> the forgiveness of sins, in accordance with the riches
> of God's grace.
> —(Ephesians 1:7 NIV)

His Blood

During my life, I had to forgive,
It wasn't easy; it took humility.
Living with hatred was no way to live.
I prayed and I pleaded, "God, please help me."

I know what his answer would be to me:
"Because of you, my Son was there,
Crucified so you could be free."
His blood is now all that I see.

When he shed his blood upon that tree,
That is what Jesus did for me.
There are no sins; they are forgiven
All—past, present, and future sin.

It is his blood that sets us free
So we could have eternity.

I can go now into God's presence.
No guilt or shame; I have been cleansed.
Jesus's blood covers me from all sin.
Without his blood, I'd be condemned.

"It is finished."

Comment on "Trust"

Every day, I find more reasons to trust him. He has proven to me that I can trust him in every circumstance of my life. I have tried trusting in myself, and it always ends in disaster. One of the best examples that I read in the Bible is that of David. He had to trust God to stay alive. The Lord always came to his aid.

I am finding out in my life that the more I trust, the more I can trust. His Word tells me that though I may stumble, I will not fall. He will uphold me with his hand. I have experienced his presence and comfort in the hardest moments of my life. But I can also say that trusting in those moments is not always easy.

I am learning to put God first in my life. I have learned when I do that, I am not alone. Whatever I face in life as I turn to him, he is there. The Holy Spirit comforts me and guides me.

> Trust in the Lord with all your heart, and do not lean on
> your own understanding. In all your ways acknowledge
> him, and he will make straight your paths.
> —Proverbs 3:5–6 (ESV)

Trust

When I trust, I can be strong,
Courageous, not afraid.
At times easier said than done—
That is when I need to pray.

You provided every time
When finances were not there.
I keep asking for a sign;
You keep proving that you care.

When tragedy struck my life
And I thought that you were gone,
I felt completely paralyzed.
You were with me all along.

After so many times
When I thought there was no way,
You were there, but I was blind.
Why do I still hesitate?

No matter what I face in life,
Whatever I go through,
Trusting you, I can survive
Surrendering to you.

How can I not trust you, Lord?
You are always there for me.
I trust in your unfailing love.
That is enough.

I am at peace.

Comment on "Gratitude"

The Bible says a lot about thankfulness. When we say thank you to God, it acknowledges that he is in control. I thank God first thing when I wake up, through the day, and before going to sleep. It is a way of life for me, ever reminding me how much I have been given.

And yet, there is so much I take for granted. I still complain when things don't go my way. Gratitude is when we can praise and thank him when everything is falling apart.

You gave your life for me. How can I not be filled with gratitude?

I had a glimpse of your glory. How can I not be filled with gratitude?

> O Lord, You are my God; I will exalt you, I will give
> thanks to Your name; For You have worked wonders,
> plans formed long ago, with perfect faithfulness.
> —Isaiah 25:1 (NASB)

Gratitude

My life is full of blessings.
My deepest gratitude,
It fills my heart. I want to sing,
Praising my love for you.

Perfect gifts come from above.
You bless me every day.
I feel the presence of your love.
You're never far away.

My soul is ever thanking you.
I want to show you day by day,
Loving others the way you do.
I know that is the way.

There is so much to thank you for:
Your mercy, love, and grace,
The Comforter you gave me, Lord—
A gift that I embrace.

My heart is full of thanksgiving.
You gave your life for me,
Loving, and so willingly.
My life you guaranteed.

To live with you eternally,
I rejoice.

God is good!

Comment on "Wisdom"

The fear of the Lord is the beginning of wisdom. True wisdom is found in obedience to God. Wisdom is a gift from God. God says that if we lack, we should ask him.

Wisdom means having the knowledge and understanding to recognize the right course of action and having the will and courage to follow it.

Why do I need wisdom? To use my knowledge to glorify him. In this journey, I have found that wisdom is the application of knowledge. Knowledge is getting to know God. Then I love him.

I have found in my life that I had to read the Bible and experience him; then came faith, and then wisdom. When I took the first step and sought him, that, to me, was the real beginning of wisdom. I found out that knowing God is what really matters—that is wisdom.

Wherever my treasure is will decide whether I have wisdom.

Blessed is the one who finds wisdom, and the one who gets understanding for the gain from her is better than gain from silver and her profit better than gold. She is more precious than jewels, and nothing you can desire can compare with her.
—Proverbs 3:13–15 (ESV)

Wisdom

Wisdom is more valuable than gold or silver.
It promises long life, honor, and riches.
"Nothing you desire can compare with her."
Her ways are pleasant. Her ways are precious.

What are the greatest riches in life?
Understanding value, understanding truth,
Peace-loving, purifying, and avoiding strife:
That is the path that I want to choose.

The Bible tells the story of Solomon.
He was given a choice; he just had to ask.
Solomon knew what mattered was wisdom.
How did he know what he had to ask?

Wisdom will show me what really matters.
My life without her would have no vision.
So many choices! I need some answers.
Help me. O Lord, my life needs wisdom.

I need to reflect: what do I treasure—
The kingdom of heaven, or this world full of pleasure?

Comment on "Peace"

What is true peace? The dictionary defines it as tranquility, security, contentment. My definition of peace would be all of the above when everything is falling apart. That is true peace.

My peace came when I was seeking God. It became real when I found Christ as my Lord. It doesn't depend on situations or circumstances around me. It is a free gift of God, just like salvation. It is something God does in my life, and I respond to it. True peace doesn't change my situation—it changes my attitude. It changes me.

I do not need to understand why things are happening to have God's peace. It is a peace that the world cannot give you. His peace belongs to me because I belong to him.

My heart did really leap. The miracle was that I was through with the Bible and ready to give up. But God wasn't through with me. He became real to me.

> The Peace of God,
> which passeth understanding.
> —Philippians 4:7 (KJV)

Peace

Your Word talks about a peace,
A peace that passeth understanding.
It seems like such a mystery!
All of life is so demanding.

I had been seeking every day.
I was about to give up hope,
But first I stopped and had to pray.
"Lord, are you there? I cannot cope."

My heart leaped, surprising me.
It happened so unexpectedly.

That was the day I felt that peace.
That was the day I felt that joy.
Your love became so real to me,
Nothing that this life could destroy.

All I can say on this long journey:
"Peace doesn't come so easily,
But you have been right there with me,
That peace no more a mystery."

The "peace of God, which passeth understanding"
(Philippians 4:7).

Comment on "Abiding in Me"

I ask myself, "When did I know for sure that I had the Spirit abiding in me?" According to the Word, it was when I surrendered my life to Jesus. At the time, I didn't feel any different, but I knew in my heart something had happened.

Months later, when I was troubled and seeking, was when I actually felt his presence. After that, I was guided to start Feed My Sheep. I knew I was in God's will. Doors opened at every turn. I would take one step forward in faith, and the impossible would happen.

I am so impressed with the many who have incredible faith and act without having any spiritual experience, but have that deep belief that can be seen in how they live their lives.

In John, Jesus said,

> *Blessed are those who have not seen and yet have believed.*
> *(John 20:29 NIV)*

God, in his grace, treats us all differently. He had a plan for me and knew I needed his presence to accomplish it.

> Then Jesus told him, "Because you have seen
> me, you have believed; blessed are those who
> have not seen and yet have believed."
> —John 20:29 (NIV)

Abiding in Me

An amazing event happened on the cross.
It is the reason Christ abides in me,
A gift so great it makes me pause
To think what happened on that tree.

The life I now live is Christ in me,
A marvel hard to understand.
God knew what he had to achieve.
His love for us—he had it planned.

I am the branch; he is the vine.
Apart from the vine, I cannot be.
Bearing much fruit is to obey.
Lord, please guide me along the way.

Glorifying God is bearing fruit,
Showing my love in gratitude.
As God abides in me
I praise and glorify you.

Comment on "Sacrifice"

The law is only a shadow of the good things that are coming. Not the realities themselves—it is impossible for the blood of bulls and goats to take away sins. Animal sacrifices were a foreshadowing of our Savior, Jesus, who was going to come as a human, having all my same weaknesses and temptations, yet he never sinned. The sacrifice had to be sinless. Only he, as the Lamb of God, could save me.

He was whipped. He was crucified. He could have stopped it at any time. He was human. He felt every lash, every nail, just like I would have. He became the mediator between God and humankind, his sacrifice offered once and for all, never to be repeated.

When I invited him into my life, it changed me. I am found not guilty. When I stand before God in judgment, Jesus will stand by me. He will be my advocate and intercessor.

> He entered once for all into the holy places, not by means
> of the blood of goats and calves but by means of His
> own blood, thus securing an eternal redemption.
> —Hebrews 9:12 (ESV)

Sacrifice

As I awake each morning,
My first thoughts are of you.
I am so filled with gratitude,
So much I want to do.

You proved how much you loved me,
A sacrifice so huge.
The one thing I can give thee is
My life in gratitude.

A life so full of flaws and sin,
And yet you paid the price:
The gift I have living within,
Your Son you sacrificed.

The Holy Spirit in me,
You shed your blood, you set it free.
Your sacrifice was not in vain.
I live to glorify your name.

No power on earth could keep you down,
Jesus Christ, my Lord and Savior,
Crucified and risen!

Comment on "Holy Spirit"

The Holy Spirit is God. He is omnipresent.

> Where can I go from your Spirit?
> Where can I flee from your presence?
> If I go up to the heavens you are there;
> If I make my bed in the depths, you are there.
> (Psalm 139:7–9 NIV)

When I accepted Christ, that Holy Spirit—that God—came and dwelt in me. Christ's disciples were ordinary people like you and me. At Pentecost, something definitely happened. When they were filled with the Holy Spirit, their lives changed. It wasn't something that happened quietly. These men were behind closed doors, full of fear. When they received the power of the Holy Spirit, what happened to their fear?

I didn't see the same results as the apostles did, but I know that I ceased being ordinary.

That same spirit that raised Jesus from the dead is the same spirit that dwells in me. It is the same spirit that will give my mortal body life.

The Bible says I am a new creation, born again. My heart's desire is to glorify and please God. The Holy Spirit changed my heart and changed my desires. It says I am sealed. I will never be forsaken.

> Therefore, if anyone is in Christ, the new creation
> has come: The old has gone, the new is here.
> —1 Corinthians 5:17 (NIV)

The Holy Spirit

The Holy Spirit abiding in me—
Your gift gave me power. The truth I can see.
It was the Spirit that changed my life—
Your love for me, your sacrifice.

What is the greatest gift God gave me?
The Word says, "Lo, I am with you always."
A comforter, a helper, leading the way,
Filling that yearning for which I pray.

It is not my effort, but Christ that achieves
The life of freedom that God has for me.
The Holy Spirit fills me with peace.
It is Christ in me.

The cross, the risen Christ, and the Spirit released:
O Lord, my God, what a great victory.

Comment on "Grace"

I read where it said grace is the most important concept in the Bible, Christianity, and the world. Grace is all around us. I see it in so many ways, starting with myself. I am alive. I am human. The gift of life is grace. Grace comes as an awareness that there is a God and that he loved me enough to die for me. Jesus is grace. I was saved by grace.

Paul said,

> For the grace of God has appeared that offers salvation to all people. (Titus 2:11 NIV)

With grace, unearned and undeserved, I am aware that I am accepted just as I am. I am loved unconditionally. Sin has no hold on me. Grace helps me to be all that God intended me to be. Christianity without grace cannot be understood.

It was grace that led a lady to my front door with a Bible. Grace is being chosen by God to be his child.

The last verse in the Bible is the following:

> The grace of the
> Lord Jesus be with all.
> —(Revelation 22:21 ESV)

Grace

It was by God's grace I was saved,
Nothing I did, nothing deserved.
I was in awe. I was amazed.
I knew something had occurred.

What did I do? What did I feel?
My first impulse was to kneel.
I felt humbled. I felt loved,
Forgiven, and not judged.

Your grace enveloped and embraced.
My heart went out to you in praise.
My whole life now belongs to you
To please in everything I do.

Although sin will be there waiting,
It will not be dominating.
Knowing grace will be with me,
I will have the victory.

Comment on "God's Forgiveness"

It used to be that when I asked God's forgiveness, instead of rejoicing, I would waste time feeling guilty. I have learned that whether I feel forgiven or not, I am forgiven. The one thing that helps me, and that I repeat, is, "If I repent and confess my sins, God is faithful to forgive me."

I refuse to let feelings dictate my life. That is the devil's job, but it is my job to watch him flee when I fight him with scripture.

God leads us to repentance. The goodness of God led me to repentance. Once I accepted him and got a glimpse of his love, my life changed. I still sinned, but my heart changed. I hate to sin, and when I do, I ask for forgiveness.

God is faithful.

> If we confess our sins, he is faithful and
> just and will forgive us our sins and purify
> us from all unrighteousness.
> —John 1:9 (NIV)

God's Forgiveness

As I was seeking to know you,
My thoughts went back to my past.
My sins I had to review.
Forgiveness was there if I asked.

I had no doubt of your love
As I searched with all of my heart.
With my sin I had hurt you enough.
Lord, forgive me! I need a new start.

I repent and know I'm forgiven.
The sorrow I feel is so real.
My forgiveness is not based on feelings;
God's promise is all I need.

When I repent and confess, I find,
Reading your Word renews my mind.

Then when something brings up my past,
I'll say, "Jesus took care of that."

Comment on "Attitude"

I have heard that life is 10 percent what happens to us and 90 percent how we react to it. My attitude determines so much of what happens every day. Anyone that I come in contact with can be changed by my attitude.

Attitude is a little thing that makes a big difference. If I develop an attitude of thanks, giving thanks to God and knowing that he is working always for my good, I learn to trust him, and that brings peace and joy.

I have talked and read about trusting God. It wasn't until the trials came that I really knew what it meant. Trusting, to me, was peace when everything was falling apart. An attitude of patience while I wait.

This verse says it all; this is the attitude that God wants for me:

> But the fruit of the Spirit is love, joy, peace,
> patience, kindness, goodness, faithfulness,
> gentleness, self-control; against such things
> there is no law.
> —(Galatians 5:22 ESV)

Attitude

My attitude determines what my day will be like.
When awakening in the morning, if my first thought is of Christ,
No matter what lies ahead, I know he'll make it right.

At times it is not easy, life can be such a fight.
My attitude determines what my day will be like.
Everyday is a choice that I alone can make
A decision I make as soon as I awake

When my life goes into chaos, as it so often does,
Will I say, "Your will be done," or will I say, "Enough"?
I know when I am tested, God is working in my life.
Maturity and growth will come about with strife.

Attitude is the key—it changes life from dark to bright.
God will take care of the rest if my attitude is right.

Comment on "Who Is in Control?"

God is the creator. Nothing happens by chance. Everything is controlled by God. I don't believe in coincidences. Even when it seemed impossible, he has provided. Instead of thanking him, I assumed I had changed the circumstances.

I look around my home, and I can see that even the things I have purchased by mistake have turned out to be exactly what I needed. I look back at the time I fell in love with a house—I just had to have it. When I tried to purchase it, everywhere I turned, a difficulty came up. I didn't get the house. Now I can see it would have been a big mistake.

I met my husband of fifty years in Venezuela. How that came about was a miracle.

The only thing I have control over is whether to obey or disobey God. What I do know is God loves me, and that gives me peace.

> And we know that all things work together for
> good to them that love God, to them who
> are called according to His purpose.
> —Romans 8:28 (KJV)

Who Is in Control?

Time now seems to rush on by.
"Where does it go?" I have to ask.
On my mind I can't rely.
Everything is such a task.

My house needs to be cleaned;
There is laundry, groceries—and the pills.
How will I get it all achieved,
Not to forget to pay the bills?

That is the way my life is
If I forget who's in control.
God's Word is clear about this:
There is no peace without you, Lord.

I don't need to struggle.
My burdens you will bear.
Instead of trying to juggle,
I'll go to you in prayer.

At times it is not easy,
But all I have to do
Is know how much you love me.
You want the best for me.

I give you all my burdens, Lord.
Please take complete control.

Comment on "I Take for Granted"

I often take my blessings for granted. Instead of thanking God for what I have, I take it for granted. Instead of being content and satisfied, I complain.

How can I tell if I am taking God for granted? By the way that I live my life? Do I ignore God? Do I ever think about him? Do I ever pray or thank him?

If the stars came out only once a year, everybody would stay up all night to behold them. We all take that for granted. And yet it is such a tremendous display of his glory and, as the verse says, the work of his hands.

Jesus shows up in my life all the time, but if I don't stay aware, I miss him. He is there providing opportunities. He is there when I have problems. He is with me, ready to help me at all times. Then when things are solved, I just assume I did a good job. That is taking him for granted.

When I pray, I feel like my prayers are too simple. Here I am addressing the creator of the universe. Then I remember the gift of the Holy Spirit. He is always with me, helping me, interceding for me. Jesus died so I would have that comforter. He nudges me. With him by my side, I cannot ignore God. I cannot take him for granted.

> On a good day, enjoy yourself;
> On a bad day, examine your conscience.
> God arranges for both kinds of days
> So that we won't take anything for granted.
> —Ecclesiastes 7:14 (MSG)

I Take for Granted

Each day as I awaken,
My first thoughts are of you.
The restful sleep you've given
I take for granted too.

The beauty that I see each day—
Sunrise, sunsets, wondrous views—
Such a beautiful display
I take for granted too.

The times that you've protected me
From sins that would my life undo—
How could I have failed to see
I took for granted too?

The times that you've provided
When all the bills were due,
The times that it was all supplied
I took for granted too.

How can I begin, Lord,
To express my thanks to you,
Thanking you for your support
In everything I do?

But most of all, I thank you, Lord,
For the way that you've changed me.
I'm not the way I was before.
Your love set me free.

I thank you now throughout the day.
I am aware of you.

Especially for your love, dear Lord—
I now take that for granted too.

Comment on "Beloved"

What a wonderful word: *beloved*. Why am I called his beloved? Not because I earned it; not because I am worthy—I sin every day. What have I ever done to deserve that unconditional love? The Bible says,

Beloved, we are God's children now. (1 John 3:2 ESV)

He loved me first. He chose me. He died so that I would receive him—the Holy Spirit. One of the hardest things for me to learn was to accept that unconditional love. Maybe it is because the world is so void of that kind of love. I may never fully comprehend the love of God, but today, I am encouraged that I am called his beloved.

I humbly accept being his beloved. Undeserved, unconditional love. I am filled with joy and gratitude.

> Beloved, now are we the sons of God, and it doth not yet appear what we shall be: but we know that, when he shall appear, we shall be like him; for we shall see him as he is.
> —1 John 3:2 (KJV)

Beloved

The God of the universe,
The same God that paints the sunsets,
The same God that made the world,
Has chosen to call me his beloved

I did not have to earn his love.
He pursued, wouldn't let me go.
I rebelled. I thought, *Enough.*
Then he called me his beloved.

I felt his love envelop me,
A love so unconditional.
I had never felt so great a peace;
I knew it was a miracle.

If I listen when I pray,
I can gently hear him say,
"You are mine"—I feel so blessed
Knowing I am his beloved.

My role in this is to be loved,
Not because of who I am,
But because of who he is.

God is love.

I am beloved. I am his.

Comment on "God's Faithfulness"

Why did it take me so long? I think back and realize he was always there. What made me finally look and know that it was all true? My first look was in the Bible, but even then, I did not look with an open heart. I remember being such a skeptic. The one thing I did right was that I kept seeking. I was about to give up. I sincerely cried out and asked, "Are you really there?"

God was faithful. I have since read in the Bible,

> *You will seek me and find me when you seek me with all your heart. (Jeremiah 29:13 NIV)*

God kept that promise, and my life changed. There is no secret. You really have to want to know him. God will be faithful to the end. I almost rejected him completely, but he would not let me go. I thank God that he did not let my heart become hardened. I would not have survived.

> I sought the Lord, and he answered me;
> he delivered me from all my fears.
> —Psalm 34:4 (NIV)

> Seek the Lord while he may be found;
> call on him while he is near.
> —Isaiah 55:6 (NIV)

God's Faithfulness

God's faithfulness keeps me alive.
I used to be so unaware.
I know now how to survive.
When I pray, I know he's there.

I didn't want to let him in,
But he wouldn't give up on me.
He just kept right on knocking,
Waiting so patiently.

He knew I belonged to him,
Chosen before time began.
He wouldn't easily let me go.
He loved me, sinning as I was.

Once I opened that locked door,
His love took over my life.
How did I miss it before?
His faithfulness was my guide.

Now I am so aware.
I see his faithfulness everywhere.
In gratitude, I kneel in prayer,
My life surrendered in his care.

Comment on "Faith"

Faith is the most vital part of being or becoming a Christian. It is a seed that is implanted in our souls when we read the Bible. In Hebrews, it says,

> *And without faith it is impossible to please God, because anyone who comes to him must believe that he exists and that he rewards those who earnestly seek him. (Hebrews 11:6 NIV)*

When I opened the Bible for the first time, the last thing I had was faith. One day, I was back in United States, reading and seeking, still with the tapes and the books from the cult that were given to me with the Bible in Belize. I gave up and threw the Bible on the floor. But before I got up, I asked God, "Are you really there?" My heart leaped. The miracle for me was that I wasn't expecting anything. I was through. God knew I needed that.

As I read the Bible, the shock of what I had been missing for so many years dawned on me. I also realized the great gift that God had just given me: the grace of God.

> For it is by grace you have been saved, through
> faith—and this is not from yourselves, it is the gift of
> God—not by works, so that no one can boast.
> —Ephesians 2:8–9 (NIV)

Faith

How did I get the faith I have today?
I studied, I asked, and I prayed.
But how did I get the faith I have today?
The Bible assured me that was the way.

It started out as a tiny seed.
A taste of your love had been revealed.
I knew in my heart that I wanted more.
I opened your Word and began to explore.

The way to Faith was through your Word.
The message was clear: you had to hear.
Faith was to know Jesus—that's what I heard.
His love, his life—faith became real.

Jesus is the perfecter of my faith,
Faith I now truly embrace.

How did I get the faith I have today?
The Bible led me all of the way.

Comment on "Your Presence"

My prayer everyday is that I may never lose the intimacy with the Lord that comes with being aware of his presence. My overwhelming longing is to maintain that awareness no matter where I am or what I am doing.

He has made his presence known to me in so many ways, but the time I was truly touched by his love, the ecstasy I felt was like a foretaste of the future that awaits me living with my Creator and Savior for eternity.

Daily fellowship and prayer is the one necessary practice in my life that helps me through the trials of living in this decaying body—in this decaying world. I have felt his love, I have felt his presence and nothing that this world throws at me can destroy the faith and the love that this fellowship produces.

God's presence above all brings me great joy and inspires my trust. I can stand firm through times of trials and testings, knowing that no matter what happens he is in control. He is for me, he loves me. If I fail like I do so often, he is there picking me up, holding my hand.

> You make known to me the path of life;
> in your presence there is fullness of joy;
> at your right hand are pleasures forevermore
> —Psalm 16:11 (ESV)

Your Presence

As I go through the day, morning or night
I am aware of your presence.
When you guide
I have your peace—I have your protection

I learn as I go through this journey of life
That my feelings are not always right
I remembered your presence when I prayed and asked;
That's when I chose to remember the past,

Your help is always on time
Yet it happens again and again
When chaos comes as it always does
I worry, I whine and I fuss

I know the way is to learn how to trust
Your presence, and love, is reason enough
Lord, help me always to be aware
Your presence is always there

Comment on "Love"

God is love. He left us a love letter. The Bible gives me love and joy and peace. I want and need to be loved. That is how God made me, how he made you. Just like his Word says that he gives us a peace that passeth understanding, he also loves us with a love that I will never understand.

When I first became a Christian, I felt I had to do something to show him that I loved him. I had to learn that his love for me is not based on performance. One day, while reading the Bible, I read,

> *This is love: not that we loved God, but that he loved us and sent his Son as an atoning sacrifice for our sins. (1 John 4:10 NIV)*

All God wants is for me to understand his great love for me. He wants to have a relationship with me. I don't have to do a thing for him to love me more. Nothing can separate me from God's love. That is what unconditional love is. I am loved.

> Your love, Lord, reaches to the heavens,
> your faithfulness to the skies.
> Your righteousness is like the highest mountains,
> your justice like the great deep.
> —Psalm 36:5–6 (NIV)

Love

Love, an emotion that cannot be explained:
It can bring such joy, sometimes such pain.
Love can bring comfort to a heart that is broken.
It can give hope without a word spoken.

I had heard about God's love for us.
I couldn't understand; why all the fuss?
Then came one day I was without hope.
"Are you really there, Lord? I cannot cope."

I then experienced what God's love is like.

There are no words that can explain.
His love made me his. I knew I was chosen,
Bathed in God's love. It felt like an ocean.

I was not seeking. I did not believe.
I had not confessed or made a commitment.
He came to me while I was in grief.
Thank you, Lord, for being persistent.

He knew—that I didn't care.
He stayed by me. Why was he there?
Knocking and waiting patiently,
Waiting to pour his love on me,

His mercy and grace a mystery.
Because of him, I have victory.
Now I understand why all the fuss.
Nothing compares to God's love for us.

Comments on "God's Timing"

I almost called this poem "Anxiety". It is about strife, which can cause anxiety. But primarily it is about waiting on God, knowing that whatever is happening will work out for our good. I can say it, I can even know and understand it, but as the difficult situation is happening, the anxiety is still there.

I want to share part of an article that I saved years ago. I have no idea where it came from. I received this when my husband was going through spinal surgery in 2011. I needed to hear it then, and I need to hear it now —I need this truth each and and every day.

> *Anxiety: don't carry it, walk with it, eat with it, live with it, go to bed with it. Don't entertain it, support it, or encourage it—not in big things or little things. It's neither a friend nor an edifier: it's a downer. It's a binder, not a freer. It will quickly introduce you to its cousins, fret and fear. Instead of being anxious about something, you can begin to pray about everything. As you pray and trust God to work, he will give you the assurance that he is in control.*

God never forgets us when we are going through hard times. I just need to remember that it is all in his timing.

Do not be anxious about anything
but in every situation, by prayer and petition,
with thanksgiving present your requests to God.
—Philippians 4:6 (NIV)

God's Timing

The situations changing; I can feel the strife begin
The day began so quietly; I don't know how it will end

I can feel my stomach churning. My mind
thinks it knows what's best
Please God resolve it my way, this way will give me rest

Hours, days, and weeks go by; a solution hasn't come;
I want it to go *my* way—dear Lord, I want it done.

I finally get so tired, I lay it at his feet
I tell him it is yours to fix, just let me get some sleep

The peace is overwhelming that finally comes to me
My mind's at rest my brain is calm, your timing's what I see

Thank you God for being here, surprising me each day
And teaching me to trust you, in strife that comes my way

Comment on "God's Will"

I have found in my life that to have true contentment, satisfaction, and peace, I must know that I am in God's will. If I truly love God, nothing else will satisfy. I pray; I ask; I seek. It is not always easy. His timing is different from mine. His ways are different from mine.

I was reading the Bible, and the words leaped out at me: "Feed my sheep." Then I saw on TV at Christmas where people were helping others in need. Why only at Christmas?

I had a picture painted of Jesus overlooking a city. I found people in need. I got addresses and started to visit. I made cards telling each person's story and what he or she needed. Those cards, along with the picture of Jesus, went into many stores and churches. The main idea was one person helping another. My only condition was that no money was to be given.

I was amazed at the way God opened doors. I would take one step, and what seemed impossible kept happening. Being in God's will is exciting.

> For all that is in the world—the desires
> of the flesh and the desires of the eyes
> and pride of life—is not from the
> Father but is from the world.
> And the world is passing away along with its desires,
> but whoever does the will of God abides forever.
> —John 2:16–17 (ESV)

God's Will

How can I know I am in your will?
My heart's desire is to please you.
I want a mission to feel fulfilled,
To show my feelings are true.

When I know I am in your will,
I feel such peace and joy.
Is it wrong, needing to feel complete,
Or pride that will destroy?

I wonder at times what direction to take.
Since I've known you, I know I can trust,
Waiting for you and living by faith.
You never fail; you always instruct.

As I walk with you, Lord, and obey,
You reveal one step at a time.
Each step I take is one of faith.
I know you have a design.

I earnestly ask in prayer every day,
Please guide and direct all my steps.
I walk out blindly. I don't know the way
But trust I will be blessed.

I am always amazed at what happens to me
Just when I think it can't possibly be.
You give me the victory.

Comment on "Eternity"

I am a child of God. My eternal life will be in heaven. I love to meditate and imagine how incredible my life will be. Thinking of seeing Jesus face-to-face, to see the one who gave his life for me, makes my heart flutter with excitement.

Living in his presence for eternity. No sin, no fear, no injustice. Only love. I lead my life thinking of eternity. No matter what happens in this life, nothing will change the glorious future that awaits me.

All God has ever done in my life has shown me how much he loves me. My part was to allow him in. It was his love that planned creation, that planned redemption, It knows no failure. Nothing will change his plan or purpose.

> He has made everything beautiful in its time.
> He has also set eternity in the human heart,
> yet no one can fathom what God has
> done from beginning to end.
> —Ecclesiastes 3:11 (NIV)

Eternity

My thoughts on eternity:
Hard to fathom how it will be.
It is a promise God gave me—
To live with him eternally.

God sent his Son, a sacrifice,
The Lamb of God; he gave his life.
A price so great had to be paid.
Couldn't there have been another way?

I can't explain or understand.
Someday it will be revealed
How God had it all planned,
When Jesus came to intercede

Thank you, Jesus, for the cross.
Without the cross, I would be lost.
When God looks down, what does he see?
It is your blood that covers me.

Life with no pain, no grief, no tears,
Age of no importance there.
Faith gives me certainty.
My life awaits eternity.

Comment on "My Savior"

My first question when I am face-to-face with Jesus will be, "Why? Why did you come down from your throne and become a human like us? Knowing what you would go through. You would be hated; you would be tortured in the most horrible way—crucified!

"What astonishes me is that at any point you could have said, 'Enough.' Legions of angels would have come to stop the crime.

"You, the God of creation, came with one mission: to save humanity. You came to show us how to live, how to love. To show us the Father. That was your true mission. You became my Savior, my mediator with the Father. You will be my advocate and intercessor when I stand before God.

"I am humbled to be loved so unconditionally. In gratitude, I surrender my life to you. I will obey and serve you with the talents you have blessed me with.

"You are my Lord and Savior."

> And we have seen and testify that the Father
> has sent his Son to be the Savior of the world.
> —1 John 4:14 (ESV)

My Savior

The God that created the heavens and earth,
He is my Lord and Savior.
I did nothing that I should deserve
Such love from my creator.

The Father sent his Son Jesus,
Knowing what would be his fate,
A human with all of my weakness.
I bow before God amazed.

He knew how helpless I was
With a sin that had to be paid.
My Savior disregarded the cost;
As a human, he came to obey.

He was crucified and tortured.
How can I ever repay
The sacrifice he offered?
Thank you, God, for your grace.

But that is not the end of the story.
His resurrection. His victory.

My Savior's alive today!

Comment on "The Resurrection"

As I was fumbling around trying to decide if there really was this all-powerful God, one thing brought me to attention. The disciples. They were surprised. Even though Jesus had told them, they were surprised.

Their belief in Jesus caused their deaths. They were human like you and me. They were tortured. They were martyred. That made me take another look at the evidence. After the resurrection, the scared disciples that were hiding behind closed doors came out completely changed. They finally knew the truth.

The resurrection is the foundation of Christianity. It was foretold hundreds of years before he was born. If I don't believe in the resurrection, I don't believe in God. He created the universe; he created life. If not God, who did?

I am sure that he who created life, who created the universe, has the power to resurrect. The resurrection proved who Jesus was.

> I am the resurrection and the life.
> The one who believes in me will live
> even though they die.
> —John 11:25 (NIV)

The Resurrection

Those three words—"He is risen"—
Give hope to a world. All is forgiven.
Some call it a mystery; I call it history.
It is the greatest of all victories.

It is written; the proof is there.
Appearing to hundreds, witnesses declared.

Jesus was sent to complete a mission—
A mission of love, a mission of mercy:
To die a death by crucifixion.
Lord, help me to live a life that is worthy.

The crucifixion, the resurrection—
They opened the way into God's kingdom.

He is my Savior.
He is alive.

Comment on "The Cross"

The cross represents Jesus's victory over sin and death. It is the greatest symbol that Christianity has. Jesus could have avoided his death, but he knew why he had come into this world. We had to have both the cross and the resurrection. The cross cleansed us of our sins. The resurrection gave us eternal life.

He had to be sinless, the Lamb of God. It was a spiritual transaction. The human race sinned; it had to be a sinless human who paid the penalty for our sins.

Someday, I hope to understand the spiritual warfare that is still going on today. Someday, I will understand what a great price Jesus paid for me and how much love he had for me.

On the cross, Jesus became the sacrifice for my sins. He did what I could not do for myself. Because of him, I have eternal life. Because he was resurrected, I know that God accepted the sacrifice. I was guilty; now I am free.

> And being found in human form,
> he humbled himself by becoming
> obedient to the point of death,
> even death on a cross.
> —Philippians 2:8 (ESV)

The Cross

Jesus was the Son of God.
He was also one of us.
He felt the same pain and sorrow
That any one of us does.

The thought of what Jesus went through
Makes my heart burn and ache—
What he went through for me and you,
The strength and love it had to take.

He could have said "Enough" at any time.
Legions of angels would have come
To put a stop to such a crime—
Then the devil would have won.

Jesus died upon that cross.
It seemed like such a terrible loss.
Not even the apostles knew
That Jesus was not yet through.

The resurrection was the proof
What he had told them was the truth.

He had arisen. He was alive.

O death, where is your victory?
O death, where is your sting?

Comment on "What Jesus Did"

What did Jesus do? Where do I start? I would start with two things—two reasons why he came.

1. To show us the Father.
2. To save humanity.

I came to understand what he had done for me when I began to read the Bible. The Holy Spirit and the Bible opened my eyes.

I feel there is a spiritual battle going on that somehow I am a part of.

Jesus did his part. There is a potential life waiting for me. I want to be a part of it. He is the example that I am to follow.

He became like me so that I would become like him. He left instructions. He left me the Holy Spirit. He left me a gift of love.

At the end of this journey, I want to hear him tell me, "Well done."

> For there is one God and one mediator between
> God and mankind, the man Christ Jesus.
> —1 Timothy 2:5 (NIV)

What Jesus Did

O Lord, what happened on that cross
That changed the world, changed history?
You knew there was no other way.
That was the price you had to pay.

We now the Holy Spirit have.
That's what you paid for—thank you, God!—
A comforter to guide us through.
My life has changed because of you.

O Lord, what happened on that cross?
You opened up the way to God.
His presence now comes from within.
That curtain tore; I can go in.

I am so filled with gratitude.
Where would I be without the cross,
The pain, the suffering you went through?
How can I make it up to you?

O Lord, what happened on that cross?
I can rejoice now I'm not lost.

How great thou art!
How great thou art!

Poems By Marcie Wert
Comments By Lissette Trahan

INSPIRATIONAL

You, God, are my God, earnestly I seek you;
I thirst for you, my whole being longs for you,
in a dry and parched land where there is no water
—Psalm 63:1(NIV)

Introduction

Although I have never met Lissette, the story of how we were brought together is, in itself, a miracle.

I send out daily devotionals and encouragements to women and men. One of the women receiving these devotionals knew Lissette and forwarded them to her. Lissette felt the need to share her thoughts on these devotionals, and through a series of emails, we were connected.

As we continued to correspond, Lissette explained that she wrote poetry. She began to send some of her poems to me. In turn, I forwarded them to a select group of women who I felt would benefit from her writings. It was when she began to write the additional commentary on the poems that her poetry took on a new, more powerful meaning. Although she and I have never met in person, we are connected by our love for the Lord and through her writings, which have touched many lives, including mine! I know that others reading these poems will be inspired and uplifted, too.

—**Marcie Wert**
February 4, 2018

Comment on "The Hole"

This poem was sent and composed by a wonderful friend, Marcie Wert, who lives to glorify God's name.

This piece says so much about our journey in life, both before and after we become a Christian. When I first read it, the words resonated in me, and I understood the truth of what it was saying. This poem made my spirit leap!

Our life here on Earth is a battle, but we are not alone. That hole, that yearning, is Jesus, who is cheering us on, telling us not to quit. Our weapon against Satan is the Word, the sword of the Spirit. Because of Jesus, we have a comforter living in us. We have the Word, which is a love letter, instructions for living, and a gift of love.

We need to open our eyes and see the universe around us; we need to read the Word with an open heart, and most of all, we need to pause and listen. As we continue to seek God, we will hear His voice—not in a whisper, but loud enough to awaken us.

Satan will continue fighting us but he has lost, Jesus won that victory on the cross.

Jesus has risen, He is alive!!

> I spread out my hands to you;
> I thirst for you like a parched land
> —Psalm 143:6 (NIV)

The Hole

When God created us, He left within us all
A tiny hole that isn't filled until we hear His call.
Until the day we listen, we grow and use our will
The hole becomes a yearning and cries out to be filled.

The hole becomes a tiny voice, one that's barely heard
But suddenly, our soul cries out; it wants to hear the Word!
Our minds are all a clutter with the sounds of our own life
We try to hear the Word but cannot because of strife.

I listen to the battle cries all through the dark, black night,
And suddenly, as dawn appears, the Word fills me with light
The voices fighting through the night, I know within my soul,
Are God and Satan fighting hard to fill that tiny hole.

The Word that we all hear, throughout our life till now
Is God's still voice within our soul that wants to show us how.
The choice is ours—it has to be—but He's always there to plead,
"Please come to me and trust me, and I will take the lead."

Comment on "Words"

Words are powerful. God created our world with words. Words can inspire or destroy. They can heal, or they can crush. The words I speak can have a huge impact on others. Once they are said, they can only be forgiven, not forgotten.

The tongue is a small thing, but it can do an untold amount of damage. Harsh words can hurt a person more than physical pain.

I try to think before I speak. Sometimes, it is best not to speak what is in your heart. The Bible says the following in Matthew 12:36–37 (ESV):

> *I tell you, on the day of judgment people will give account for every careless word they speak, for by your words you will be justified, and by your words you will be condemned.*

That verse revealed to me the power and consequences of my words. Idle words can condemn me? That makes me stop and think before speaking. I will be judged by my words because they reveal the state of my heart. It was with words that I received my salvation. It is words that I use when I confess my sins.

Words have a weighty influence in our eternal destiny.

> Let the words of my mouth and the
> meditation of my heart be acceptable
> in your sight, O Lord,
> my rock and my redeemer.
> —Psalm 19:14 (ESV)

Words

I don't think she meant to hurt me
I know this deep inside
But the feelings that I have in me
Are very hard to hide

Was she really trying to help me
Or was she trying to hurt?
Was what she said really true,
Or something I deserved

I want to do what's right and good
And if her words were true
Help me God to change them
To something you can use

Help me to apologize;
Help me change to be
The person you created
Let others see you in me.

Comment on "Unforgiveness"

I can relate to this poem. I remember the hateful thoughts, the torture, that I put myself through. I could feel it ruining my health, and yet I wouldn't let go. I could not do it on my own.

But. . . when I turned and asked God to help me, I was able to forgive and even apologize to her and to God, for how I had been acting. The actual act was not easy, never excusing myself or asking for explanations. My flesh screamed to tell someone how she had hurt me, but that would not have been forgiveness.

Was it worth it? The feeling of release and freedom that I felt was an act of God. My bitterness and resentment—the poison that was eating away at me—disappeared. Unforgiveness was replaced with the peace that God promises in His Word.

I realized that the Father would not forgive my sins unless I forgave others. Once I let that knowledge sink in, I was ready to forgive. I sin every day, but the thought of God not listening to me, not forgiving me, I could not bear.

After that experience, I became quick to forgive. It isn't easy—in fact, it hurts quite a lot—but the benefits are tremendous.

Forgiveness is an act of obedience. Like Marcie says in her poem, don't carry that rock: let it go.

> For if you forgive other people when they sin against you,
> your heavenly Father will also forgive you.
> But if you do not forgive others their sins, your Father
> will not forgive your sins.
> —Matthew 6:14–16 (NIV)

One Defining Moment

One defining moment in each of our lives
That make our life have purpose, that make us feel alive

One defining moment which way before our birth,
God has a plan for each of us so we may feel our worth

One defining moment we fit into his plan, the one we were
created for, there's one for every man...

Sometimes when we are open, we can be truly blessed,
To know that one small moment, which brings us happiness

One defining moment—or two, or three, or more
If you're open to the master's call, and do not his Word ignore

Sometimes we are open, but even if we're not
God uses us to help another fill their special spot

So on the days you wonder, why you have been brought here,
That one defining moment will help to make it clear.

Comment on "The Purpose"

Life can be complicated. We all need a purpose, a goal, a reason for getting up in the morning. My life used to be without meaning.

When, exactly, did my life change? It started to change when I read the Bible for the first time. But the real change happened when I continued seeking God, yearning to know Him with all of my heart. His Word says,

> *You will seek me and find me*
> *when you seek me with all your heart.*
> *—Jeremiah 29:13 (NIV)*

I used to wonder, like Marcie, "What is this life all about? Why am I here? Why all the suffering, abuse, and injustice?" There are some questions that don't have answers. But this I know: God is faithful, and I can count on His promises. He will never leave me nor forsake me. Life without Him has no meaning. He gives my life purpose.

> And we know that in all things God works
> for the good of those who love him,
> who have been called according to his purpose.
> —Romans 8:28 (NIV)

The Purpose

Sometimes we travel through our life
And think our purpose clear
We think that money, work or fame
Will be our main career

The day comes to all who live
We find that work does cease
We look back at what mattered then
Hasn't given us much peace

What then is my main purpose
And where is my mistake
What matters in this life, I ask
And is it now too late?

Is all in vain? Do I matter?
It isn't very clear
Why was I born? I do not know...
Why else would I be here?

There is a voice in each of us, we don't give it a name
The voice that tries to tell us that these things are all in vain

Sometimes if we sit and listen to the voice inside us all
The voice that tries to talk to us will reveal himself and call
"I am your purpose in this life. It's me that you must choose;
If you surrender all to me, your life you'll never lose"

I will not give you easy paths, I will not promise fame
It might be full of grief, or sorrow and sometimes even pain
What I promise is an inner peace, a kind you've never known
Whatever you are going through, you'll never be alone

My name is Jesus, and though it's frightening now
My Spirit who abides in you will always
Teach you how

Comment on "The Mother That Was"

What I remember about my mother is that she loved me. She wasn't perfect, but what parent is? I knew that no matter what I did or what happened she would always love me.

Did she always think of how her actions would affect me? No, but she loved me. She was always there for me at my most crucial moments. I look back now and see how God protected me. He kept me safe and I always felt loved.

Could I have had a better childhood? Absolutely. She followed her heart, she followed her husband, the man that she loved to Venezuela.

I am glad she did, but it did disrupt my schooling and my life as a child. I regret now the times I didn't love her back as she deserved.

In this life a mother is to be treasured and cherished, she won't be here forever.

"Honor your father and your mother"
— which is the first commandment with a promise —
—
—Ephesians 6:2(NIV)

The Mother That Was

The mother I knew died so long ago
In my heart I've always loved her so

I remember her cleaning, cooking and such
But other than that she didn't have much

She wasn't a joiner or doer per se
I can't remember her smiling much in those days

When the grandchildren came she seemed to smile more
She would laugh at their jokes and antics for sure

For a moment in time I saw what could've been
And I wish I could have held the moment but then...

She hadn't been perfect, but she was so giving
She just didn't have a passion for living

I wish I could have known how to bring her to life
So maybe her life wouldn't have had so much strife

Mom, you're finally at rest and I hope now you know
How much that I loved you deep down in your soul

I want to remember the woman that was:
The grandmother, mother, wife and the friend...
The one that I loved and will miss till the end

I hope you're at peace — the mother I've loved
I will always miss the mother that was.

Comments on "The Skit"

This metaphor is so true in life. I know I play roles all the time. I tend to say what I think a person wants to hear. Why? I think we all need to be accepted, and we all need to be loved. The part I play depends on the circumstances. It has become a habit that I am not even aware I am doing.

The devotion I received today was about how much God loves me. Nothing I do or say can reverse that. That should be all that matters. I don't need to play a part. My main part in this life should be to love others and to obey God at all times.

This poem was a good reminder that failing is part of life. I ask for forgiveness, get back up and with his help start over.

> Love must be sincere. Hate what is evil;
> cling to what is good.
> — Romans 12:9 (NIV)

The Skit

From the moment you are born to life there is a part you play
Sometimes it is for someone's good, sometimes leads them astray

Sometimes you do auditions for the part that you will play,
You know the lines, you rehearse them well, you'll know just
what to say

At other times, you are the one, that is the one who's used
You sometimes play the other role, the one who is abused.

Sometimes you are the hero – you help and you are kind
Sometimes you play the villain – and mess up someone's mind

In life, God knows the parts you'll
choose – He gives us all free will
You find yourself in different parts and some you do with skill

There is a lesson to be learned from the skits in life you play
Choose the very best director to guide the words you'll say

We look at life quite different now...we know we have a choice
To choose the role and do it well and use the master's voice.

Comments on "The Cry of the Soul"

This poem by Marcie Wert is a must-read. It will touch the many souls of persons going through the same crisis. Though problems in life may seem to have no solution, there is an answer. God came to her rescue as he will do with anyone who cries out to him.

All of us reach times of despair. I did when I lost my son. I also turned in despair and cried out to God. He answered and turned my sorrow into joy. God treats each of us differently, and it is always his timing, not ours,but he is never late.

I am so grateful to Marcie for sharing this poem with me. I offered to make the author anonymous, but she said

"You can put my name on it...as you know the writings are not ours...they are given and inspire".

That is so true and beautiful. My wish, my passion is that this book will bring people closer to God. That they will see how real he is. When that knowledge sank into my soul, my life changed.

Of all the poems in this book I consider this one the "masterpiece".

In my distress I called to the Lord;
I cried to my God for help.
From his temple he heard my voice;
my cry came before him, into his ears
Psalm 18:6(NIV)

134

The Cry of the Soul

The night is black my mind is too, I know I'm at the brink
All I want to do is end my life, my mind won't let me think

Help me God to do what's right, what is this thing I face?
Why can't I get beyond myself? Why can't I win this race?

What is this that is stopping me, why can't I hear you speak?
I need to know that I'm okay. Please help me God—I'm weak!

Why do I feel so all alone? Why can't I feel your love?
I need you Lord to help me, please protect me from above...

Please listen child and hear me speak,
I'm here with you and know
That what you're going through right now, a battle for your soul

So don't listen to that voice that speaks, the one that says to die
Come to me and give your life I hear your frightened cry!!

The battle isn't easy, it isn't meant to be,
But all you do is call on me and I will set you free

You have the power deep inside to fight this evil voice,
It's important to remember it will always be your choice!

Each person that is born on earth will face this very call
Some will choose to follow me, others will choose to fall

The battle started in the garden with Adam and with Eve...
When Satan came and tempted them and started to deceive

That's why I had to come to earth to die for all mankind
But the battle rages until the end, the battle for the mind

The purpose of your life on earth is to choose to live for me
But Satan will always tempt you, he doesn't want you free

So place your faith and trust in me the battle will be mine
Just call my name, and believe and see,
that peace will soon reside

Printed in the United States
By Bookmasters

Unforgiveness

What is unforgiveness? It's heavy and it's cold
The damage that it does to us is like a rock we hold
What matters if I keep the rock? Who cares how much I hate?
The wrong that has been done to me, it wasn't a mistake...!!!

It isn't for that person that forgiveness needs to be;
It's for your inner spirit and the way to set you free
If you don't let go of this, it will bring you down:
You cannot grow, you cannot love, your spirit is now bound.

So anyone you can't forgive, just give them all to Him;
He will take the hurt you feel and heal you from within.
I promise you'll feel better if you do this from the start:
And love and peace will fill the space of hatred in your heart.

The action that you need to take is simple, and it's clear
Write the names, and say a prayer, and leave them all right here.
The fireplace is the perfect place to take the step you need
To rid yourself of the rock you hold, and your spirit will be freed

Comment on "One Defining Moment"

I remember my one defining moment. I was living in Belize, and I had opened a Bible for the first time. I remember being interested in it, but I was still a skeptic. My first prayer was a plea to God during my first tour in Belize: "I want out of this jungle. Help me find a way back to the U.S."

He answered my prayer. We came back to a beautiful home, and I started a ladies accessory shop. I was living the American dream. I kept reading the Bible, seeking for answers, knowing that there was so much that I needed to learn. I was frustrated, the cult said one thing, the Bible said another. I kept seeking.

One day, something happened. It is hard to put into words. I didn't hear his voice or feel his touch, but I felt His presence—I felt His love.

A silent voice said to me, "I am with you always." Silent, because the words I heard did not come from me; I did not know that the verse was in the Bible. And at the same time, my heart leaped. All of this was unexpected.

That was my defining moment. I have since had many moments with the Lord, but that was the first. I became a believer, and after feeling that loving presence, my whole life changed.

Do I still sin? Yes, but that voice that I heard, "I am with you always," makes me run back to Him and confess. My defining moment was almost 50 years ago. In all that time, He has been faithful, even when I wasn't.

> You will seek me and find me
> when you seek me with all your heart.
> —Jeremiah 29:13 (NIV)